CAMBRIDGE PRIMARY
Science

Skills Builder

T0159736

Jon Board and Alan Cross

CAMBRIDGE
UNIVERSITY PRESS

CAMBRIDGE
UNIVERSITY PRESS

University Printing House, Cambridge CB2 8BS, United Kingdom

One Liberty Plaza, 20th Floor, New York, NY 10006, USA

477 Williamstown Road, Port Melbourne, VIC 3207, Australia

314–321, 3rd Floor, Plot 3, Splendor Forum, Jasola District Centre, New Delhi – 110025, India

79 Anson Road, #06–04/06, Singapore 079906

Cambridge University Press is part of the University of Cambridge.

It furthers the University's mission by disseminating knowledge in the pursuit of education, learning and research at the highest international levels of excellence.

www.cambridge.org
Information on this title: www.cambridge.org/9781316610985

First published 2016

20 19 18 17 16 15 14 13 12 11 10

Produced for Cambridge University Press by
White-Thomson Publishing
www.wtpub.co.uk

Editor: Rachel Minay
Designer: Tracey Camden

Printed in Spain by GraphyCems

A catalogue record for this publication is available from the British Library

ISBN 978-1-316-61098-5 Paperback

....

Contents

Introduction	**4**
1 Being alive	**5**
1.1 Animals and plants alive!	6
1.2 Local environments	7
1.3 Animal babies	8
1.4 Healthy food and drink	10
2 Growing plants	**11**
2.1 Plant parts	12
2.2 Growing seeds	14
2.3 Plants and light	17
3 Ourselves	**20**
3.1 We are similar	21
3.2 We are different	23
3.3 Our bodies	25
3.4 Our fantastic senses	26
4 Materials in my world	**28**
4.1 What is it made of?	29
4.2 Using materials	31
4.3 Sorting materials	33
5 Pushes and pulls	**35**
5.1 In the playground	36
5.2 How toys work	37
5.4 Changing movement	39
6 Hearing sounds	**40**
6.1 Where do sounds come from?	41
6.3 Sounds move	42
Answers	**44**
Glossary	**48**

Introduction

This series of primary science activity books complements *Cambridge Primary Science* and promotes, through practice, learner confidence and depth of knowledge in the skills of scientific enquiry (SE) and key scientific vocabulary and concepts. These activity books will:

- enhance and extend learners' scientific knowledge and facts
- promote scientific enquiry skills and learning in order to think like a scientist
- advance each learner's knowledge and use of scientific vocabulary and concepts in their correct context.

The *Skills Builder* activity books consolidate core topics that learners have *already* covered in the classroom, providing those learners with that extra reinforcement of SE skills, vocabulary topic knowledge and understanding. They have been written with a focus on scientific literacy with ESL/EAL learners in mind.

How to use the activity books

These activity books have been designed for use by individual learners, either in the classroom or at home. As teachers and as parents, you can decide how and when they are used by your learner to best improve their progress. The *Skills Builder* activity books target specific topics (lessons) from Grades 1–6 from all the units covered in *Cambridge Primary Science*. This targeted approach has been carefully designed to consolidate topics where help is most needed.

How to use the units

Unit introduction

Each unit starts with an introduction for you as the teacher or parent. It clearly sets out which topics are covered in the unit and the learning objectives of the activities in each section. This is where you can work with learners to select all, most or just one of the sections according to individual needs.

The introduction also provides advice and tips on how best to support the learner in the skills of scientific enquiry and in the practice of key scientific vocabulary.

At this grade, it is very likely the learners are still learning to read, so teacher/parent may need to explain these verbally.

Sections

Each section matches a corresponding lesson in the main series. Sections contain write-in activities that are supported by:

- Key words – key vocabulary for the topic, also highlighted in bold in the sections
- Key facts – a short fact to support the activities where relevant
- Look and learn – where needed, activities are supported with scientific exemplars for extra support of how to treat a concept or scientific method
- Remember – tips for the learner to steer them in the right direction.

How to approach the write-in activities

Teachers and parents are advised to provide students with a blank A5 notebook at the start of each grade for learners to use alongside these activity books. Most activities will provide enough space for the answers required. However, some learner responses – especially to enquiry-type questions – may require more space for notes. Keeping notes and plans models how scientists work and encourages learners to explore and record their thinking, leaving the activity books for the final, more focused answers.

Think about it questions

Each unit also contains some questions for discussion at home with parents, or at school. Although learners will record the outcomes of their discussions in the activity book, these questions are intended to encourage the students to think more deeply.

Self-assessment

Each section in the unit ends with a self-assessment opportunity for learners: empty circles with short learning statements. Teachers or parents can ask learners to complete the circles in a number of ways, depending on their age and preference, e.g. with faces, traffic light colours or numbers. The completed self-assessments provide teachers with a clearer understanding of how best to progress and support individual learners.

Glossary of key words and concepts

At the end of each activity book there is a glossary of key scientific words and concepts arranged by unit. Learners are regularly reminded to practise saying these words out loud and in sentences to improve communication skills in scientific literacy.

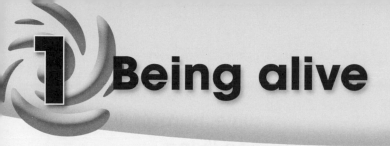

1 Being alive

The activities in this Skills Builder unit give learners further practice in the following topics in the Learner's Book and Activity Book:

Topic	In this topic, learners will:
1.1 Animals and plants alive!	identify living and non-living things
1.2 Local environments	sort animals and plants in a local environment
1.3 Animal babies	name the young of different animals
1.4 Healthy food and drink	sort healthy and unhealthy food

Help your learner

In this unit, learners will answer questions by collecting evidence through exploring and observing (Section 1.2). They will also start to make comparisons (Sections 1.1, 1.2 and 1.4). To help them:

> ! Learners will need adult help in Section 1.2 to keep them safe.

1 In Section 1.2, look up the names of the animals and plants with learners and help them to write these as labels on their drawings.

2 In Section 1.3, research a baby animal with learners in more detail using books or the internet. Research is a useful scientific enquiry skill.

3 Look up the key words for the unit with learners in the Glossary and talk about what they mean before learners do the activities.

1.1 Animals and plants alive!

alive, human, living, non-living

Living or non-living?

1 Is it **alive**? Draw a line from each picture to the right word.

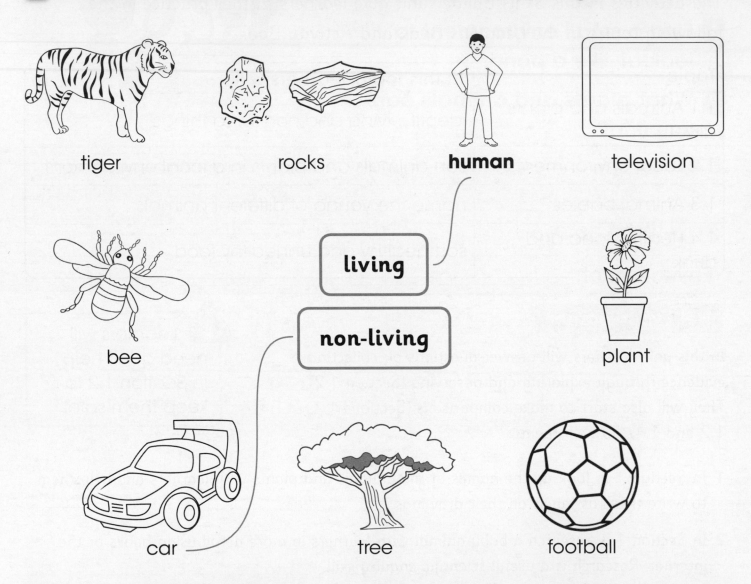

tiger

rocks

human

television

bee

living

non-living

plant

car

tree

football

2 Colour the living things.

CHECK YOUR LEARNING

○ I know if something is alive or not.

1.2 Local environments

magnifying glass, environment, plant, animal, compare

What lives here?

*You will need a **magnifying glass**.*

1 Find a small **environment** to look at, like a pond.

2 What **plants** and **animals** can you find?

! Only look in safe places. Look out for plants that sting or animals that bite.

Draw them here:

Environment: _____	
Plants	Animals

CHECK YOUR LEARNING

◯ I can look closely and **compare** animals and plants.

1.3 Animal babies

baby, cub, calf, chick, name

Whose baby?

Join each animal to its **baby**. Write what the baby is called.

cubs

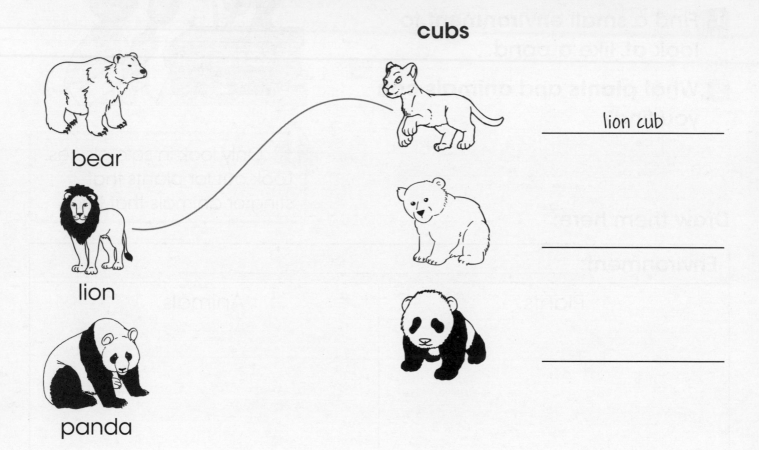

bear

lion

panda

lion cub

_____

_____

elephant

cow

whale

penguin

chicken

parrot

calves

_____

_____

_____

chicks

_____

_____

_____

CHECK YOUR LEARNING

◯ I can **name** some baby animals.

1.4 Healthy food and drink

A healthy lunch

1 Draw arrows to put **healthy food** into Leon's lunchbox.

2 Colour in the healthy foods.

3 Draw your favourite healthy snack.

CHECK YOUR LEARNING

◯ I know which foods are healthy.

2 Growing plants

The activities in this Skills Builder unit give learners further practice in the following topics in the Learner's Book and Activity Book:

Topic	In this topic, learners will:
2.1 Plant parts	name the different parts of a plant
2.2 Growing seeds	predict the way a plant will grow and compare this with the growth of an actual plant learn that seeds need water to grow
2.3 Plants need light	understand that plants need light to grow

Help your learner

In this unit, learners will suggest ideas and follow instructions (Sections 2.1, 2.2 and 2.3) and practise exploring and observing in order to collect evidence (Section 2.3). They will also make and compare predictions (Section 2.2) and make comparisons (Section 2.3). To help them:

1 Encourage learners to ask questions and answer them by making observations.

2 Help and supervise learners to handle materials.

TEACHING TIP

It is very important that learners draw things they observe, but you can also take digital photographs to help.

! Remind learners that some plants are poisonous.

TEACHING TIP

On a walk around the school or home, ask learners to observe plants, the parts of the plant and whether the plants have enough water and light.

roots, stem, leaf, flower, fruit

Finish the picture

1 Safiya needs help to finish the picture. Draw the other side of the picture for her.

LOOK AND LEARN

Plants have **roots**, **stems** and **leaves**. Some have **flowers** or **fruit**.

stem

leaf

flower

roots

2 Draw a line to join each label to its plant part.

Think about it!

3 Look at the finished picture.

    a How many stems are there? _____

    b How many leaves are there? _____

    c How many flowers are there? _____

CHECK YOUR LEARNING

◯   I know that plants have roots, stems and leaves.

◯   I know that sometimes plants have flowers or fruit.

My growing seeds

You will need a plant pot, seeds, soil and water.

1 Sow some **seeds** in soil, in a plant pot. Give them a little **water**.

2 Put them near a window and look at them each day.

3 Draw a picture as soon as you see the seed start to **grow**. Count this as Day 1.

My drawing on Day 1

4 Draw what you think the plant will look like on Day 7.

What I think the plant will look like on Day 7

5 Wait until Day 7. Draw your plant.

My drawing on Day 7

Plants need water

Look at the plants below. Draw lines to show which plants have enough water.

Just like people, plants need water.

This plant has enough water.

This plant does not have enough water.

CHECK YOUR LEARNING

○ I know that plants need water to grow.

Plants need light

Hannah has been growing bean plants.
Circle the sentences that are right.

Remember:

Plants need lots of **light** to grow well.

| The plants by the window have enough light. | The plants on the floor have enough light. |

| The plants by the window don't have enough light. | The plants on the floor don't have enough light. |

Plants love the light

You will need a plant in a pot.

1 Put a plant near a window but not close to the glass.

2 Draw your plant each day. Does it grow towards the light?

Day 1	Day 2

Day 3	Day 4

Day 5	Day 6

Day 7	Day 8

3 **Think about it!**

We need sunlight to keep us well, but we don't grow towards the light. Why not?

_____

CHECK YOUR LEARNING

◯ I know that plants need light to grow.

3 Ourselves

What learners will practise and reinforce

The activities in this Skills Builder unit give learners further practice in the following topics in the Learner's Book and Activity Book:

Topic	In this topic, learners will:
3.1 We are similar	understand that people are similar in lots of ways
3.2 We are different	understand that people are different in lots of ways
3.3 Our bodies	name the main parts of the body
3.4 Our fantastic senses	learn about the senses and test their friends' eyesight

Help your learner

In this unit, learners will collect evidence through observation to answer questions (Sections 3.1 and 3.3), and make comparisons (Section 3.2) and predictions (Section 3.4). To help them:

1 Be aware that learners often find it easier to see differences than similarities. Remind them that we all breathe, eat, hurt, cry, have hair and skin, and so on.

2 When making the eye test (Section 3.4), learners may need to think about ways to make it a fair test, for example not allowing their friends to see the eye test before they use it.

TEACHING TIP

The senses are important so encourage learners to use the words to describe them. Talk together about your senses and the senses of other people and animals.

3.1 We are similar

similar

Ways we are similar

1 **Look at the children. Tick all the sentences that say the children are similar.**

We all love toys. ☑

We all have hair. ☐

One girl has hurt her arm. ☐

We are all children. ☐

We can all smile. ☐

2 **Look at the boy and the man. They are different sizes. In what ways are they similar?**

They both have _____

_____

_____

CHECK YOUR LEARNING

I know that we are similar in lots of ways.

Differences I see

1 **Draw yourself and three friends.**

In what ways are your friends different from you?

Remember:

We can have different hair, skin, eyes, clothes. We can like different foods and games.

Me	Friend 1
	is different from me because
	_____
	_____

Friend 2	Friend 3
is different from me because	is different from me because
_____	_____
_____	_____

2 **Think about it!**

Can you think of other ways you are different from your friends?

_____

CHECK YOUR LEARNING

◯ I know that we are different in lots of ways.

3.3 Our bodies

> body, head, hair, eye, ear, mouth, nose, shoulder, arm, fingers, hand, knee, leg, toes, foot

10 fingers? 20 fingers?

You will need to work with a friend.

1 Look at the key words above. Can you point to each part of your **body**?

2 With a friend, count your body parts. Fill in the chart.

On my body I have	Together we have
_____ fingers	_____ fingers
_____ eyes	_____ eyes
_____ legs	_____ legs
_____ ears	_____ ears

3 **Think about it!**

Can you name other body parts, like your chin or your cheek? Write them here.

_____

CHECK YOUR LEARNING

◯ I can name the main parts of my body.

3.4 Our fantastic senses

Make an eye test

You will need a big piece of paper and four friends.

This is an eye test. The letters at the top are big and the letters at the bottom are very small.

Your sense of **sight** is good if you can read the small letters.

LOOK AND LEARN

Our **senses** tell us about the world around us. We can **see**, **hear**, **smell**, **touch**, and **taste**.

1 Make your own eye test. The letters need to get smaller as they go down.

2 Now test four friends. How many do you think will see the smallest letters?

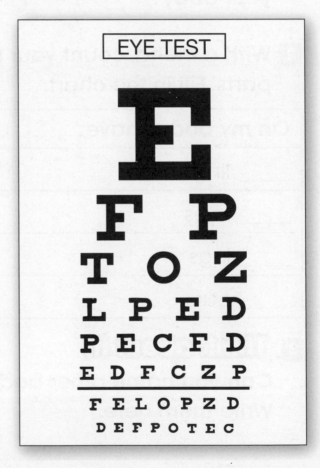

EYE TEST

E
F P
T O Z
L P E D
P E C F D
E D F C Z P
F E L O P Z D
D E F P O T E C

_____

3 Ask your friends to stand ten steps away. Show them your eye test. Can they read all the letters?

_____

4 How many can see the smallest letters? Were you right?

_____

Animal senses

1 Draw a line to match the animal with its best sense.

KEY FACT

Some animals have amazing senses.

see

smell

touch

hear

2 **Think about it!**

A whale can hear other whales over 100 km away. What would it be like if you could hear other people that far away?

_____

CHECK YOUR LEARNING

◯ I know my senses tell me about the world.

◯ I know that animals have senses and some animals have amazing senses.

4 Materials in my world

What learners will practise and reinforce

The activities in this Skills Builder unit give learners further practice in the following topics in the Learner's Book and Activity Book:

Topic	In this topic, learners will:
4.1 What is it made of?	look closely at and name different materials
4.2 Using materials	recognise that different materials have different properties explain why different materials are used for different jobs
4.3 Sorting materials	sort materials based on their properties

Help your learner

In this unit, learners will collect evidence to answer questions (Sections 4.1 and 4.3), decide what to do to try to answer a science question and record stages in work (Section 4.3). They will also communicate ideas in order to share, explain and develop them (Sections 4.2 and 4.3). To help them:

TEACHING TIP

Talk with learners about why different materials are used for different jobs.

1 Materials are usually made into objects. Encourage learners to talk about the properties of the material rather than the object, for example a towel is made of soft cotton, an iron is made of strong metal.

2 Help learners to carry out investigations. Always ask them to predict what will happen, observe what does happen and then try to explain what happened.

4.1 What is it made of?

materials, metal, plastic, wood, rock, fabric, rubber, paper, glass, concrete

Materials all around

You will need a magnifying glass.

1 Find some different safe **materials.**

2 Use the key words to help you name the material.

3 Look at the material carefully through the magnifying glass. Draw what you see.

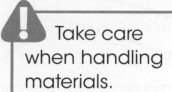

⚠ Take care when handling materials.

The material is ___fabric.___

I can see holes. _____

_____

_____

_____

The material is _____

_____

_____

_____

_____

The material is _____

_____

_____

_____

_____

The material is _____

_____

_____

_____

_____

4 **Think about it!**

Some things are made from more than one material. Look at a pencil case, or school bag. Can you find different materials? What are they?

_____

CHECK YOUR LEARNING

◯ I know that there are lots of different materials.

◯ I can name some different materials.

pet, properties, soft, see-through, strong, smooth, flexible

The right material

1 Look at the materials in the **pet** shop. Use these words to finish the labels.

| glass | fabric | straw |
| metal | plastic | wood |

sand

concrete

paper

2 Draw lines to match the object to the **properties** of the material.

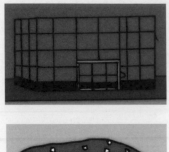

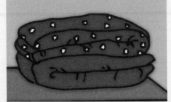

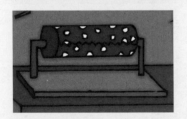

a pet's cage   **soft** and **warm**

a pet's blanket   **see-through**

a glass tank   **strong**

wrapping paper   **smooth** and **flexible**

3 **Think about it!**

The door of the pet shop is made of wood and glass. It is not made of paper. Why not?

_____

CHECK YOUR LEARNING

◯ Different materials have different properties.

◯ Materials with different properties are used for different jobs.

Sorting machine

This machine is **sorting** objects. Say which box each object will go into.

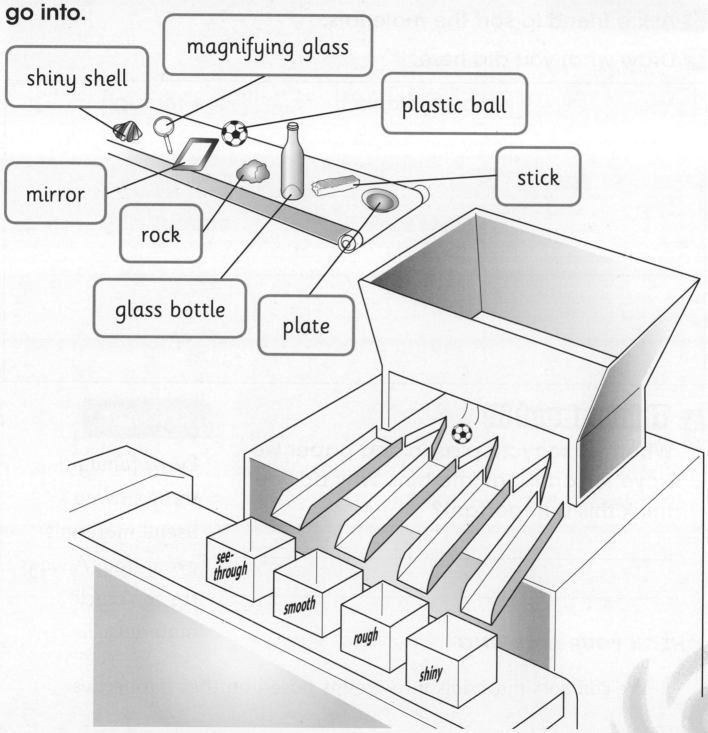

shiny shell

magnifying glass

plastic ball

mirror

stick

rock

glass bottle

plate

see-through

smooth

rough

shiny

Make a sorting game

Make a sorting game for a friend.

1 Make three labels for properties.

2 Choose some safe materials.

3 Ask a friend to sort the materials.

4 Draw what you did here.

5 **Think about it!**

When we **recycle** plastic and paper we have to sort them into bins. Why do you think this is important?

_____

_____

KEY FACT

Every family throws away useful materials every day. Always try to recycle materials.

CHECK YOUR LEARNING

○ We can sort materials into groups based on their properties.

5 Pushes and pulls

What learners will practise and reinforce

The activities in this Skills Builder unit give learners further practice in the following topics in the Learner's Book and Activity Book:

Topic	In this topic, learners will:
5.1 In the playground	describe different ways of moving
5.2 How toys work	identify that pushes and pulls can cause movement
5.3 Pushes and pulls around us	see Challenge, Section 5.3
5.4 Changing movement	compare the effects of big and small pushes

Help your learner

In this unit, learners will explore and observe in order to collect evidence to answer questions (Section 5.2). They will also make comparisons (Sections 5.2 and 5.4). To help them:

1 In Section 5.4, talk with learners about the 'Think about it!' question. This will develop their skills of considering evidence.

2 In Section 5.4, some learners could be challenged to use fast, faster and fastest and slow, slower and slowest.

! Make sure that learners do not push or pull things that are too big or heavy and might cause damage to objects and people.

run, jump, swing, turn, move

Different ways of moving

1 Write these words with the right picture.

run   jump   swing   turn

_____   _____   _____   _____

2 **Think about it!**

Which is your favourite way to move?

_____

CHECK YOUR LEARNING

◯   I can name different ways to move.

push, pull

Pushes and pulls, right or wrong?

1 Are these pictures in the right place? Put a tick or a cross in each box.

Remember:
There are different ways of moving but they all need a **push** or a **pull**.

Push

Pull

Push	Pull
☐	☐
☐	☐
☐	☐

2 Draw a picture of something that moves when you push it.

Push

3 Draw a picture of something that moves when you pull it.

Pull

CHECK YOUR LEARNING

◯ I know that pushes and pulls can make things move.

fast, slow, faster

Fast!

Big push, small push

You will need a toy car and a ball.

1 Push the toy car and the ball with a big push, then a small push.

2 Do they go **fast** or **slow**? Write it in the table.

big push ➡	small push ➡	big push ➡	small push ➡
fast or slow?	fast or slow?	fast or slow?	fast or slow?

3 **Think about it!**

Which push makes things go **faster**? Tick one box.

big push ☐

small push ☐

CHECK YOUR LEARNING

◯ I know that bigger pushes make things move faster.

6 Hearing sounds

What learners will practise and reinforce

The activities in this Skills Builder unit give learners further practice in the following topics in the Learner's Book and Activity Book:

Topic	In this topic, learners will:
6.1 Where do sounds come from?	identify sources of sound
6.2 Our ears	see Challenge, Section 6.2
6.3 Sounds move	compare loud and soft sounds learn that sounds move away from the source

Help your learner

In this unit, learners will practise making comparisons (Sections 6.1 and 6.3) and exploring and observing in order to collect evidence (Section 6.3). To help them:

1 Some learners will describe sounds as 'big' or 'small'. Encourage these learners to use the more scientific words 'loud' and 'quiet' or 'soft'. Some learners might be able to use 'loudest' and 'quietest' as well as 'loud', 'louder', 'quiet' and 'quieter'.

2 In Section 6.3, encourage learners to listen very carefully to the quiet sounds with and without the listening tube. This will be easier to do in a quiet place without other noises.

! Take care with the 'Listening tube' activity (Section 6.3). Very loud sounds can damage your ears.

TEACHING TIP
Encourage learners to close their eyes when listening to sounds. This will help them to concentrate more on what they hear.

Spot the sound source

1 Colour in only the pictures that are sound sources.

LOOK AND LEARN

A **sound source** is something that makes a sound.

2 **Think about it!**

Are you a sound source?

yes   no

CHECK YOUR LEARNING

I can spot a sound source.

Listening tube

You will need some thin card and some sticky tape or a card tube

⚠ Take care. Very loud sounds can damage your ears

A listening tube makes sounds louder. The sound moves through the tube.

1 Make the tube and then listen to some soft sounds through it.

2 Draw three sound sources. Do they sound louder or **quieter** through the tube?

My sounds		
louder ☐ or quieter ☐	louder ☐ or quieter ☐	louder ☐ or quieter ☐

Think about it!

3 Which sound was the quietest?

_____

4 Which sound was the loudest?

_____

CHECK YOUR LEARNING

◯ I know that sounds move.

Answers

1 Being alive

1.1

Living or non-living

1

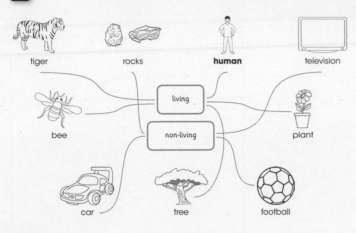

tiger   rocks   **human**   television

living

non-living

bee   plant   car   tree   football

1.2

What lives here?

1 to **3** Answers will depend on the environment chosen and the plants and animals seen. Plants should be drawn in the plant column, animals drawn in the animal column.

1.3

Whose baby?

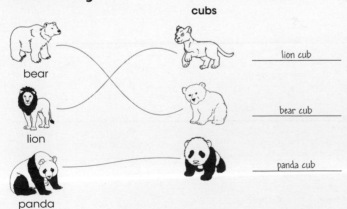

cubs

bear   lion cub

lion   bear cub

panda   panda cub

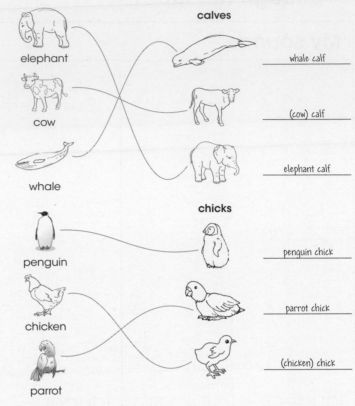

calves

elephant

cow

whale

whale calf

(cow) calf

elephant calf

chicks

penguin

chicken

parrot

penguin chick

parrot chick

(chicken) chick

1.4

A healthy lunch

1 and **2** The learner should have coloured in the milk, tomatoes, sandwiches and bowl of rice and vegetables. They should have drawn arrows from these foods into the lunchbox.

3 The learner should have drawn a healthy food or drink in the box.

2 Growing plants

2.1

Finish the picture

1 and **2** The learner should have finished the drawing of a plant with roots, stem, leaves and flowers. They should have joined the labels with lines to the correct parts of the plant.

Think about it!

3 The learner will count the stems, leaves and flowers.

2.2

My growing seeds

3, **4** and **5**

The learner will have drawn their plant on Day 1, a prediction for Day 7 and a picture of the actual plant on Day 7.

Plants need water

This plant has enough water.

This plant does not have enough water.

2.3

Plants need light

The learner should have circled these sentences:
The plants by the window have enough light.
The plants on the floor don't have enough light.

Plants love the light

2 The learner should have made a diary of drawings which show the plant or its leaves turning towards the light.

3 Think about it!
Learners may explain that we don't grow towards the Sun because we are not green, we move around, we are not plants. Accept any reasonable statement.

3 Ourselves

3.1

Ways we are similar

1 Learners should have ticked these four boxes:
We all love toys.
We all have hair.
We are all children.
We can all smile.
Learners should not have ticked: One girl has hurt her arm.

2 Correct answers include any way that the two pictures are similar, for example they are both boys, they both love soccer, they are both wearing kit and boots, and so on.

3.2

Differences I see

1 The learner should have drawn themselves and three friends, and written notes about the ways they are different. Answers can refer to bodily features such as hair and eye colour, pastimes and sports they like or dislike, or indeed any reasonable response.

2 Think about it!
The learner might talk about differences in their body or appearance or about their behaviours, habits, hobbies or pastimes.

3.3

10 fingers? 20 fingers?

1 The learner should point to their own body for each of the key words at the top of the page.

2 The table will be complete with numbers for the learner and their friend. For example:

On my body I have	Together we have
10 fingers	20 fingers
2 eyes	4 eyes
2 legs	4 legs
2 ears	4 ears

3 **Think about it!**

The learner might list a number of body parts.

3.4

Make an eye test

2 , **3** and **4**

The learner should record their prediction and whether the prediction was right.

Animal senses

1

2 **Think about it!**

The learner might talk about conversations across 100 km, for example it would mean they could talk to friends anywhere in town and around, which would save the cost of phone calls. They might realise that they could hear everyone within 100 km and that this would be very difficult and noisy!

4 Materials in my world

4.1

Materials all around

2 and **3**

The learner should have named their materials and drawn them as they appeared under the magnifying glass. They should write some descriptive words about the appearance of the material. This is a flexible activity so there are many correct responses.

4 **Think about it!**

The learner should be able to look at an object made of different materials and identify some of the materials. For example a chair might be made with wood, metal and fabric.

4.2

The right material

1

2 The learner should have drawn lines as follows:
a pet's blanket to soft and warm
a glass tank to see-through
wrapping paper to smooth and flexible

3 **Think about it!**

The learner should explain why paper is not suitable. For example because it is weak, it would get wet if it rained and fall apart, thieves could get in, animals could escape. Accept any other sensible reason.

4.3

Sorting machine

The materials should be sorted into:
see-through – glass bottle, magnifying glass
shiny – mirror, shell
smooth – plastic ball, plate
rough – rock, stick

Make a sorting game

4 The learner should have recorded what they did.

5 Think about it!

The learner might talk about the need to collect the plastic together so it can go to the factory that makes the plastic bottles. This idea would apply to other materials to be recycled. Encourage any reasonable answer.

5 Pushes and pulls

5.2

Different ways of moving

1

| jump | run | swing | spin |

2 The learner should have recorded a way that they like to move.

5.2

Pushes and pulls, right or wrong?

1

Push	Pull
✓	✗
✗	✗
✓	✓

2 The learner should have drawn a picture of something that needs a push here.

3 The learner should have drawn a picture of something that needs a pull here.

5.4

Big push, small push

2

big push	small push	big push	small push
fast or slow?	fast or slow?	fast or slow?	fast or slow?
fast	slow	fast	slow

3 Think about it!

big push ✓

6 Hearing sounds

6.1

Spot the sound source

1 The learner should have coloured in only the television, truck, guitar, aeroplane and cat.

2 Think about it!

yes ✓

6.3

Listening tube

1 and **2**

Answers will depend on the sounds chosen. All sounds will sound a little louder through the listening tube.

3 and **4 Think about it!**

Answers will depend on sounds chosen.

Glossary

alive	something that is living
animal	a living thing that can move around and eats other living things
baby	the young of an animal
calf	a baby cow, elephant or whale
chick	a baby penguin, parrot or chicken
compare	look at how things are similar and how they are different
cub	a baby lion, bear or panda
environment	a place where living things live
food	what animals eat
healthy	good for you
human	men, women and children are humans
living	living things grow, need food, make waste, use air and have young
magnifying glass	shaped glass that makes objects look bigger
name	say what something is called
non-living	not alive
plant	a living thing that can make its own food

Remember:

Practise saying these words aloud. Try to use them when talking about the topic.

flower

fruit

leaf

stem

roots

grow	get bigger
light	brightness from the Sun; plants need light
seed	the part of a plant from which a new plant can grow
water	liquid that plants need to grow

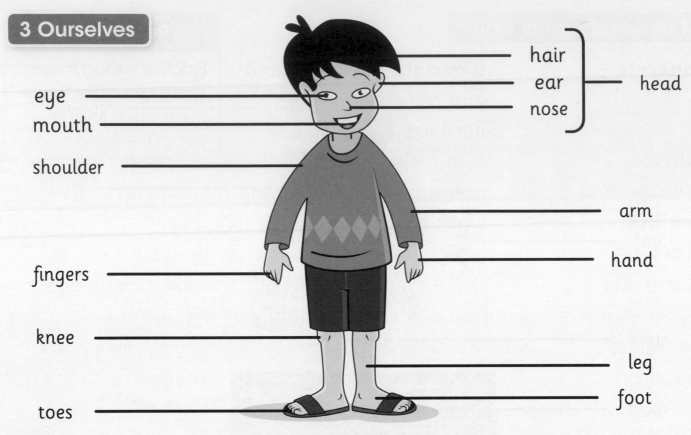

eye
mouth

shoulder

fingers

knee

toes

hair
ear
nose
head

arm

hand

leg
foot

body	the whole part of a person or animal
different	not the same
hear	you hear sounds using your ears
see	to look at things with your eyes
senses	the things animals use to find out about the world around them
sight	you use your eyes to see things
similar	being the same in some ways
smell	you use your nose to smell things
taste	you taste your food and drink using your tongue
touch	a sense you use to feel things

concrete	a mixture of water, sand and cement that goes hard like a rock
fabric	a soft, flexible material used to make clothes and other things
flexible	when something can bend easily
glass	a material that you can see through
materials	we use materials like glass, wood, plastic and fabric to make many things that we use every day
metal	a material that is often strong and shiny
paper	a material that you use to write on
pet	an animal that you keep in the home
plastic	a type of material that may be coloured
properties	the words we use to describe a material
recycle	use a material again
rock	hard material found in the ground
rough	bumpy, not flat
rubber	a material that can bend easily and keeps water out
see-through	clear or very thin so you can see through it, like glass
shiny	looks bright when light shines on it
smooth	flat, not bumpy
soft	gentle to touch, not hard
sort	put things into groups
strong	powerful, not easily broken
wood	a material that comes from the trunk of a tree

Remember:

Practise saying these words aloud. Try to use them when talking about the topic.

5 Pushes and pulls

fast/er/est	taking a short time to get to another place
move/ing/ment	change position
jump	move so that you are not touching the ground
pull	try to move something away from you
push	try to move something towards you
run	to move your feet quickly, faster than walking
slow/er/est	taking a long time to get to another place
swing	to move backwards and forwards, as on a swing
turn	change direction

6 Hearing sounds

listen	you use your ears to listen to sounds
loud/er/est	a sound that makes a lot of noise
quiet/er/est	a sound that does not make much noise
soft	a quiet sound
sound	something you hear
source	where something comes from or where it is made